LAUNCH A GREAT BUSINESS

BUSINESS

TOP 10 WAYS TO MAKE YOUR COMPANY SOAR

Doug Thorpe

Limits of Liability / Disclaimer of Warranty:

The authors of this information and the accompanying materials have used their best efforts in preparing this course. The authors make no representation or warranties with respect to the accuracy, applicability, fitness, or completeness of the contents of this course. They disclaim any warranties (expressed or implied), merchantability, or fitness for any particular purpose. The authors shall in no event be held liable for any loss or other damages, including but not limited to special, incidental, consequential, or other damages.

Table of Contents

Table of Contents

Launch a Great Business.. 1

Top 10 Ways to Make Your Company Soar.. 1

Limits of Liability / Disclaimer of Warranty: 2

Table of Contents 4

Introduction 6

Chapter 1: Today Isn't Everything, Really 9

    Think About This 11

Chapter 2: Set the Goal Now, For Tomorrow's Benefit............................. 13

    How to Set Goals Successfully 14

Chapter 3: Growing And Staying Green 18

    The Long Term Goal... 19

    Enter The Car Manufacturing Business 19

    How To Do It... 21

    Understanding the Ever Changing Consumer.................................... 22

Chapter 4: Understanding Your Market... 25

    To Consider Now... 26

    Paying Attention Counts 28

Chapter 5: Trend Versus Trend Setter... 30

    Long Term Trend?.. 31

    Consider Your Reputation 32

Chapter 6: Principal: History.. 35

    Questions to Consider 36

    All Histories Are Not Bad 38

Chapter 7: Investing In Knowledge.. 40

    A Principle.. 41

    Making It Count... 42

    Making Wise Choices.. 43

    Decision Making Tips 44

Chapter 8: Growth Success without Potential Waste.............................. 47

It's Personal Too 48

Growing Too Fast.. 49

Are You Ready To Grow?... 50

Don't Limit It 51

Chapter 9: Managing Money Principles 53

Controlling Your Money, Correctly 54

Don't Think You Need To?.. 56

Your Cash Flow.. 57

Two Principles to Remember 59

It's Not Being Cheap, It's Being Smart.. 60

Chapter 10: Marketing For True Success.. 64

Determine Your Product's Potential 65

Pricing Matters Too 66

Marketing Effectively 68

Sales for Success 69

BONUS RECAP CHECKLIST... 72

BONUS #2... 74

Conclusion.. 77

Introduction

What does being an entrepreneur mean to you?

Anyone that is interested in finding true success throughout their lives can do so, with the right tools, the right amount of ambition and the knowledge to make it all happen. Yet, the entrepreneur, no matter which business he is in he must plan ahead and find success through much more than just these things.

To be an entrepreneur, you are not just looking for benefits right now. While you are sure to want your business to truly take off and do well in its first year, its infancy, it is just as important, if not more so, that the long term goals that you have match the need that you have as well.

In the long term, the entrepreneur's world is much different and much more unique. To find true success, he needs to think of today as well as tomorrow-two fold.

How and what will you do to insure that your business, the one that you have worked so hard to make happen in the first place, is going to make it in the long term? Although this is not something easy to do, you can do it with skill.

In this book, you will learn some of the most essential principals of protecting your business not only for today, but also for the long term.

As a new or aspiring entrepreneur, you did not think about what the future would hold because only today mattered. Yet, now is the perfect time to step back and to find out just what the best way to manage your business sin the long term is.

If you wish to have a business that allows for success and money in your pocket down the road, it is essential that you spend some time now planning for it to happen.

The good news is that you do not have to go to school or be a rocket scientist to figure this out. In fact, we provide a great deal of the information and resources that you need here, without any need to look elsewhere.

Of course, we also hope you are inspired to take the next step and to find the true benefit of your business by putting these things into action first and foremost. When you do these things, true success and money in your pocketbook is all that will matter.

Chapter 1: Today Isn't Everything, Really

As an entrepreneur, your job is very detailed. You need to be the creative one. You need to be the boss. You need to hold the vision of your business at the head of each and every thing that you do for that business. But, today isn't everything.

As a business owner, you must remember the fact that the long term goals and process of your business can only happen if you plan for it now, not in the day.

You have probably heard people tell you that you need to; "Live in the day!" As an entrepreneur, this is not possible and should not be the way that you hold your business agenda.

But, why not?

Most of the time, we would like to think that all we really need to do is to put together a plan and hold onto it. Somehow, things will fall into place. It has to. That's all it can do.

Yet, from a business standpoint, there is much more to think about.

For example, you may have employees that need the funds that come from your business for their day to day expenses.

You may need to take into consideration the overall benefits that you have in keeping your business going. What about your assets? Will they make it through the process? How about your cash flow? What will happen if something does go wrong?

All of these things are really only the tip of the iceberg when it comes to ruining a business in the long term. The bottom line is that you need to consider what your business will be like today as well as ten, twenty and more years down the road.

Before we get started, it is essential that you understand two concepts of your business dealings. When you make a decision in your business, ask yourself these questions first and foremost.

1. When I make this decision, what is the short term and immediate effects of doing so? How does this affect my business today?

2. When I make this decision, what is the long term effect of making this choice? How will this decision affect my business months and years from now?

When you take the time to carefully consider decisions that happen in front of you, you put yourself in charge of your destiny.

If you allow the cards to fall where they may, you may not be in business six months from now. Therefore, as you work through this book, ask yourself what steps you can take right now that will better your overall business in the short and the long term.

Of course, we should mention that there is never a for sure way to know what the future holds. There is no way to know if you are really making the right decision or not. But, what you have to do here is to insure that you give tomorrow the best possible chance that you can.

Don't let it just happen, make today count for tomorrow and tomorrow's tomorrow too.

Chapter 2: Set the Goal Now, For Tomorrow's Benefit

No matter what aspect of your life you are talking about, goal setting is a crucial factor throughout it all. As you will see, each of the decisions you make as an entrepreneur will affect your overall goal of being successful with your business. Yet, there is more to it than just that.

You should also set goals because they can help you to make the right decisions throughout the process of getting to the level of success that is coming. By investing the time and energy that you have in setting goals now, you help yourself for each decision it takes to reach the end result you are hoping for.

In other words, if you set some overall goals today, you can help insure that your business will be there and be prosperous throughout the future of the business. Goals now, count.

While we all have the same goal of finding success in the future, we still need to set goals to help us to get to that point. It doesn't happen overnight!

How to Set Goals Successfully

When it comes to setting goals, there are not many of us that are very good at doing so. There are plenty of opportunities for mistakes to be made, but the real problem comes in how we set them as well as what we do once we set them.

For starters, it is essential to know what your goals are. Take a few minutes right now to figure this out. Simply sit down with a blank sheet of paper (yes, you can use your computer too!) and avoid all distractions for ten minutes.

Write down anything and everything that comes to your mind in regards to your goals.

- What are they?
- Where do you want to be in a year?

- Who do you want to have with you? Where do you see your business in five years? 20?
- What dollar amount of sales will make you happy this year?
- What do you need to make in profits to reach a new level of satisfaction each year?

All of these things may be things to spark your mind. Determine where your business will be within the next years. Look long term for starters. Then, follow these tips.

Goal writing is made easy through some basic steps.

1. Write down your longest term goal. This is the place that you want to be in a number of years, or the place you need to be to be as successful as you plan to be.

2. Give yourself a time frame for making that happen. You may want to say that you want to make your first million in two years. Or, it may take many more for that to happen. Giving your goal a timeframe helps to get your mind set in

how to make that happen. If you leave it open ended, the long term goals are not benefited by your actions each day, as they would be here.

3. Give yourself smaller goals to reach as steps up to the larger one. For example, the new entrepreneur may be able to say that he wants to be in an office, set up and running within a month's time. In six months, he plans to be running into profit, after expenses have been paid down. Determine what your steps are to reaching your goal. Make sure that you write them with time frames attached too.

4. Now, write them by hand on paper in the following manner. "Within six months, I will have paid off all debt that I owe and be running in the clear. I will do this by pushing sales and not pushing any new expenditures during that time." In this manner, you have listed not only what the goal is and the time frame to have it done, but also how you will get there.

5. Take this piece of paper and place it everywhere and anywhere that you will see it at least several times per day. Seeing it will allow you to think it.

Thinking about it makes it happen. Success through goals is the only way to find it.

Now that you know what your goals are, it is essential for you to make sure that they do happen.

You will need to read those goals each day, at least one time per day. When you think it, see it, feel it, you make it happen.

Throughout the next chapters we will discuss what long term decisions you need to make as well as what various things you need to do to make them happen.

When you go through each step, determine your goal for it. How will you implement it into your current work day and how will you insure that it will happen?

Chapter 3: Growing And Staying Green

When you are green, you are growing. Once you start to turn red, you are expiring. Don't you want to always stay green then?

As an entrepreneur, one thing that you should realize is that the world never stays the same. You are, for the most part, always going to find some changes happening. As a business owner, if you can not adjust your business to those changes, you may find yourself facing more problems then benefits.

Many companies have had to go out of business simply because their product no longer works with what the consumer needs. It does not matter what type of business you have either. The bottom line is that if you are not green and growing, you are not going to make it in business for long.

Is your business green and growing?

The Long Term Goal

The long term goal of any business situation is to insure that they are able to meet the needs of the client or consumer. If they can not do this, they can not have consumers and will eventually fall out of the scope. If they do happen to do this, they will find rewards continuously with increased profit and new customers to fill their pockets.

In this case, the long term goal that you need to make is to maintain green. You need to maintain some aspect that will continuously help you to move forward with what is happening within your business.

If you are not sure why this is important, take for instance, the current situation.

Enter The Car Manufacturing Business

Today, we hear quite a bit of talk about energy cost, the cost of gas and all that goes with it. In fact, today, more people know what the cost of a barrel of crude oil is than they ever have. Why is this; and what does this do for the industry?

If you haven't spent any time shopping or a car, you may not realize that many manufacturers are struggling to stay in business. Their problem is that their cars, trucks or anything in between are not able to meet the demands of the consumer.

Why not? They may not be able to offer low enough mileage. With each passing year, more and more consumers are looking for a better way to fuel their energy needs. That comes in the way of cars that are hybrids and those that do not run on gas at all.

In these cases, if the business can not meet the needs of the consumer, how can they run effective businesses?

They can't and that is the same thing that can happen to virtually any business out there. Unless your business can be green, growing and exploring new routes to take, it can not meet the needs of the consumer who is, of course, the lifeblood of the business.

The question that you need to ask yourself, then, is what do you need to do to make this happen in your business?

Let's say that you have an internet business. Perhaps one of the important things that you must do is keep up with search engine optimization.

If you do not follow and keep in contact with the new rules and the changing scheme of matters, your website won't rank well and will fall out of the scope of being worthwhile.

In this case, it is essential that you maintain the ability to keep your knowledge and your skill at the highest quality. The same goes for various other businesses including those such as insurance agency and real estate agency. Unless you keep your knowledge at the top, you can not make sure you are doing what is right.

There are other ways that you need to think about this as well. For example, what about marketing? If your marketing is not trendy enough (or happens to be too trendy for the wrong market) you may find yourself in trouble.

In this case, it is essential for you to find a way to target the right audience with the right medium and to keep it up. You already know how to market your business; just make sure that you stay up to date on how to do this as the market changes.

What other aspects of your business can you think of that have the same potential for your attention?

Finding the various ways that you need to stay fresh may include keeping your business product fresh, with the latest technology and aspects to fit the consumer's need and even reinventing yourself to insure that the company always stays at the top.

When you invest time and money into keeping yourself green, the business always has the potential for success.

Understanding the Ever Changing Consumer

One of the most difficult things that you will need to do as an entrepreneur is to insure that you meet your consumer's needs. What is difficult about this is not the fact that you need to do it, but rather how you go about understanding your consumer.

Some companies spend millions of dollars on research each year to insure that their product or that their sales pitch will be well received by the economy. The scary factors is that even with all of that, they are still risking a lot and often they do fail at what they are doing.

This can leave the small entrepreneur left to wonder how in the world they can afford to make this happen.

Understanding the consumer is not an easy task. It is essential that someone work hard to finding this information though.

If you are interested, you can do this through hiring a company to do your marketing research. This can be a solid decision that is provided at a decent cost to you. Depending on your specific business and your product, as well as your marketing budget, this may be a good option for you.

On the other hand, it may not be something that you wish to pursue. In that case, it is essential that you invest some time in finding the right solution through other means. No matter what you do from talking with your customers individually to watching market trends in what your competition does, the goal is to insure that you keep offering the best product possible.

To make sure that you are green, compare what you have to offer to the consumer's other choices. What do they have that makes them a better choice over you?

When you can answer that and then tackle that, you will be green and growing, growing towards profits of course.

Chapter 4: Understanding Your Market

One thing that we do need to mention is hat the market that you face is likely to be much different than the market that someone else faces. The goals that you have in comparison to the goals of someone else are much different. In fact, you are sure to see yourself striving for benefits that are not on target for your business.

First off, take a step back, out of the picture and look at your market.

If you are selling on the internet, look at the other sellers. If you are a small local business owner, step back and look at your local market.

Whatever you are doing, step back.

The market that you work in is very dependant on who your customers are. If you are looking for immediate success, just opening your doors can help you to get started. But, in looking at your market, you can better see several things.

Ask yourself and answer these questions before moving forward.

- Who is my customer? The seniors or the children, the business women or the business owner...determine who your customer is.

- How do they find you? Do they find you online, through a simple web search? Do they need to find you through an affiliate link? Do they find you in their local area, in one of the most popular areas in the city?

- Who else is out there? Who is your competition? Where are they located? What do they offer that allows you to better them? How do they better you in your marketplace? Why are they open, pulling business away from you?

- What do you offer that is better, in some way, then the other guy? What do they offer that is better in some way than you?

- Where is your market going? Is the economy growing, stalling out, or is it holding steady? What amount of money do your customers have to spend on your product?

You can go on and on with things that you should be considering about your own specific business. Understanding your market is crucial to understanding what your future is.

If you do not know who your consumer is, then how do you know how they are changing?

In addition, you need to know what to expect to get from the market around you. If you find that the economy is slipping, it may be quite necessary to pull back and to instead look to the future in a different way.

If you look at your market and see that your competition has taken your product in a different way and is having success with that, you need to make a move. How do you compete? What will you offer that is better? In addition, how will you take the next step into success? How will you better them?

Paying Attention Counts

By paying attention to your market, you will make better decisions. When you look towards the long term goals that you have in place to keep your business up and running, you need to make sure that your market is one of the top priorities that you have.

If you do not invest time in keeping yourself in that marketplace, or even expanding out of it, you can not and will not make things work. The business can not grow or stay green without a constant watchful eye on the market around you.

In later chapters we will talk more about growth and how to envision your future in this regard. Yet, it is important to note that you need to watch your market for the signs that it needs more of your product or that it is not picking up on it.

There is no doubt that some of these things are essential to do but some may be hard to do as well. Yet, if you do not invest the time that it takes to analyze and understand the customer that you have, how in the world will you make it work?

Again, you have the ability to hire someone to do this work for you. But, you can and you should consider not only doing this but also helping yourself with your own research and know how.

Being a physical presence in your marketplace (even on the web) helps you to make sure that people can come to you. It allows you to see your market first hand and therefore make good decisions.

Chapter 5: Trend Versus Trend Setter

Is your business a trend setter? Or, do you follow the trend?

If you are not sure, consider how this plays a role in your future.

As a trend setter, you are always one step ahead of the game. What you do, others look up to, but not just this one time. If you can manage to do this often, setting the trend that is, you can even create the fact that you will have others looking to you to set the next trend.

On the other hand, if you are following the trend, things are not so great. You will have to make up time for the other product or business that is doing well. You have lost precious sales time in the process. In addition, you will always need to watch the other guy for what is going to happen next, instead of being in charge of what that is. This can be a challenging place to be, actually.

Take a minute now to think about where you are in this equation.

Do you tend to follow the lead of someone else, hoping that there will be enough in the pot for you too? Or, do you seek out something new and exciting and try to incorporate that into your business?

Depending on where you stand currently should help you to see just how this affects your long term goals and ability to reach the success that you want.

Long Term Trend?

We all know that trends come and go. You should also realize that not every one of them is the right way to go for each business. Yet, the trend is something to pay attention to when looking at your long term success.

As we mentioned, the benefits of setting the trend in your market place are not just based on the basics of the sale. Sure, if you can get a monopoly on a product for a few days, weeks or longer, you are going to have some awesome sales to take advantage of.

Yet, those sales are soon gone. In the short term, that is all that matters. But, in this case, we are talking about the long term goals here.

If you are the trend setter, then, your long term benefits of being in this business is that you have more ability and movement to set the next trend too.

Some companies in the market place do not have the ability to fill their customer's needs perfectly. Some will only find success once in a while when it comes to trends. Yet, the company that is able to set a few trends can secure more ability in the future to do the same.

When a company has other companies looking to them for the next trend, guess who is going to make long term success?

Consider Your Reputation

This is the one factor that plays a role in developing your reputation as a company as well. Not all companies are able to say that they have a good reputation with their consumers on a long term basis. Yet, those that do can almost count on a monopoly in their market.

Take for example the mom and pop shops that are so frequently around well past their prime. Why are these such great places to go? It's because they have a solid reputation for providing success and for doing well with their product. Even if their product is outdated, it is still something that is wanted and needed for its quality. That helps to fund true success with the market.

Of course, your reputation comes into play for more reasons or ways than just this. The fact is that it also happens when you are considering customer service, pricing, good community connections and so on. These things all play a role in what your reputation is, just to name a few of them!

When you are considering your long term goal of success and having good money in your pocket, how does your reputation play a role?

We talked about how this happens with trend setting, but it can go further than that. In today's offline world, it is hard to get a good cup of coffee without begging.

No matter if you are online or offline with your product, though, you can gain many rewards and benefits by just providing good service.

Building a reputation is essential to continued growth. Yet, remember that a reputation can go both ways (good and bad!) Therefore, make sure that you have a solid backing of pleased customers in your marketplace. It will pay off for you today as well as long into the future.

Chapter 6: Principal: History

One thing that many business owners do not take into account enough is their history and learning from it. When you consider how your history affects your future potential, you can better see why it is essential for this to be something you pay a good amount of attention to.

Do you learn from history?

Many of us will recall the times when our parent's scolded us. "Don't do that again!" "Learn from your mistakes." All of these things are very important in the business world as well.

In this principal that is crucial to your business's success, you do need to take into consideration your past and where it has been to help you to figure out where you and your business are going.

Now, to get started with this principal, take into consideration these questions.

1. Where have you been and what have you learned? When you think about the past, determine just what it means to find success in this way. What background do you have that has taught you something that could play a role in your life and well being today?

2. What have you learned from mistakes? Every entrepreneur makes mistakes as they are working through their business. No matter if you are brand new or a seasoned pro, mistakes can happen one time for many reasons. But, the difference is if you allow it to happen again. If not, then you can find success much easier and faster than if you repeat the same mistake time and time again.

3. What do you wish you would have done differently? Regrets do not have to be wasted this time. As an entrepreneur, you may have several

regrets in mind. Perhaps you feel as if you have lost a great deal of time getting your business up and running. Now, take this regret and determine what you would do today. Would you start your business sooner? Put more into it sooner?

Understanding these aspects of your past can help you in the long term. Of course, we do not want to keep making the same mistakes, but there are not many business owners that do this.

Instead, most of us will learn from our mistakes but only if we take the time to look at them and see what they were and how they could be avoided.

Your history is solely yours. Whether you look at a personal life history and your business or just the business alone, it is essential to stop and look and learn.

Making mistakes today is not easy to do. No one wants to do it, but if it does happen to you, do the following.

1. Recognize that something did not go right. Do not get angry about it (if possible!) and realize that something went wrong.

2. Determine what it was and determine how it happened. Getting the full story, learning the whole puzzle will allow for better understanding. Learning how it happened allows you to see in full detail what the mistake was.

3. Decide to improve your chances of not letting that mistake happen again. To do this, insure that you spend the necessary time making decisions to avoid this problem.

All Histories Are Not Bad

It is important to note that history does not always have to tell you the bad side of things. You can and you should see the good things that have happened in your history as well. What was it that got you to this success level that you are at today? What was it that makes that first sale happen and happen so well?

Taking a look at the good things that have happened in the past is part of the principal of looking to the past for answers of your future. They allow you to see a true benefit to the good that has happened in your business.

You may even be able to take note of the way that the good has happened to make it happen again and again into your business's future as well.

When you take the time to analyze all of the good and the bad that has happened in your past, you can make sure that the benefits come through in the future while the mistakes do not.

As part of your future success, you must understand your history and how to secure the future through this huge amount of knowledge that you have. Believe it or not, this is a personal touch and experience no one else can have.

Chapter 7: Investing In Knowledge

If you are like many entrepreneurs, then you know that it is essential to have a good deal of knowledge when it comes to running your business.

As we have talked about, it is important to make sure that those that are providing you with the necessary information are doing so without taking all of your money just so that you can spend more.

For example, some of the most common mistakes the entrepreneurs that are just starting out make is that they just keep purchasing information. This is especially true of those that are starting a business online.

There is no doubt that you do need to have a good amount of knowledge to make something happen. You need to know how to get started, you need to know what steps to take and you need to know just where to do all of this. But, there is a limit.

One thing that you should take into consideration is your ability to make decisions. Once you have purchased the latest tell all kit, realize that you are ready to make some decisions.

If you purchase one kit or program and see another that seems to offer some additional benefits, you may be tempted purchase that one too. After all, it can not hurt to have some more information, can it?

It doesn't hurt to have a good amount of information, except for the pocketbook, of course. Yet, that is not the problem. What the problem is what you do with it.

A Principle

There are a number of things that you can do to make this happen to you. Remember this principle.

If you find yourself purchasing one product after another product, you are not thinking about your next productive move, but rather holding yourself up.

If you purchase a product to benefit your business, it is essential for you to use it and get the most out of it prior to moving on to the next purchase.

Making It Count

In later chapters we will talk about the fact that you need to manage your money closely, but for now, realize that the investment in any asset or tool to benefit your business needs to be used fully for it to be a wise investment.

No matter what business you are in, if you do not take the time to invest in a business product wisely, you are literally throwing your profit out.

If you fall victim to all of those ploys to purchase this great kit or that sure fire method of making a million dollars, you sure are helping someone else to make that million dollars.

Now, that is not to say that you shouldn't purchase any of them. Instead, select the one that provides the best resources for you, invest in it wisely and then use it completely, incorporating all that needs to be incorporated into the plan.

When you do this, your investment is beneficial to your business. If you just move on to the next thing, you find yourself facing not benefits but pitfalls and an empty wallet to go with it.

Making Wise Choices

In our next chapters, we will touch on some very important assets including your cash flow. But, before we do that, we need to touch on the principal of making the right decisions regarding your business.

How do you make decisions? Do you make spur of the moment choices because that is the way that you feel that day?

Do you work hard at finding the right solution, so much so that by the time you make the decision it is too late?

If you do these things, you are not benefiting your business, but rather letting the cards fall where they will. This is a huge problem for the overwhelming majority of those entrepreneurs out there that are just starting out. Making wise decisions is not easy, but it must be done, nevertheless.

Once you realize the way that you are currently making a decision, you can begin to correct it. To help you to make the right choices, follow these steps and tips to securing the right decisions without letting them get past you.

Decision Making Tips

Making a decision is hard work. Here are some tips to help you.

1. Invest time in learning about the possible product or problem that you are facing. If you are trying to decide on whether or not to purchase a product, consider what it will do to enhance your business's performance. What can it do for you?

2. Spend some time researching possible solutions, both what you have found and what you have not. What can it do for your problem? What is the

lowest cost you can find? What are the potential pitfalls of this item?

3. After this is done, determine if the investment is worth it to your own well being or to your business's. Waiting until after you learn more about the product will allow a decision to form as a conclusion to the research you have done.

4. If you can not decide within a few days, then perhaps you are too leery of this item or choice to determine it is right for your business. Let it go and forget it. Or, find another option. Do not dwell on it.

Making the right decisions also means that you need to realize your current state of affairs.

If your business is not pulling in profits because it does not have the necessary tools, it is time to invest in some new tools otherwise your business will not be there long enough for you to worry about it.

If your business is doing okay and there is no hang up, then do not invest in something that does not have a direct return on your profit margin.

Most entrepreneurs have tons of people coming to them offering them a wide range of different benefits, products, and services because, like you, they are looking to make their business work. Don't fall for these lures and savvy businessmen that think they can solve your problems.

Although it may seem difficult to make good decisions in relation to the business that you have, it is imperative that you learn to trust yourself. If you do not trust your decisions, you can not run a business.

This too is a principal that you need to realize: If you do not trust yourself, you can not ruin a successful business.

Chapter 8: Growth Success without Potential Waste

One of the long term things that every business owner must think about is growth.

Growth is the expansion of your business to the next level. This could mean expanding your business to include more products, to do more things, or to grow physically by adding more locations.

Growth is what holds the potential for the most success in the long term. An entrepreneur can find many benefits for themselves if they can manage to grow carefully, without going too far or stretching too thin too fast.

If that sounds difficult to do, it can be. Many businesses have failed by expanding too quickly and not having enough of the market share to hold them together. On the other hand, there are plenty of businesses out there that have not grown as much as they could and now are missing out on the potential larger profit margin.

It's Personal Too

Of course, the growth of your business is a personal choice. Not everyone can determine where they lie here at the beginning of their business as well. Yet, one thing is sure.

Your growth potential has a lot to do with your security in your business. If you have trust and assurance that your business is a business worth existing, then by all means you can grow. If you are not sure and can not make decisions regarding the growth of your business, it can not possibly grow.

Although most people are ready and willing to take full advantage of an opportunity to build on what they have created, others are quite willing to let the pieces fall as they may.

One principle that you need to remember, then, is that to become successful in your business, you need to determine your level of security in risk. What are you comfortable with and how can you insure that what you are doing is what will pay off in the long term?

These are hard questions to answer but they must be done.

Growing Too Fast

One of the worst things that you can do for your business is to grow too fast. If you do not have the assets and the cash flow to back up this type of major expansion, you may find yourself facing a number of problems just maintaining your business rather than worrying about expanding it.

The risk of failure due to over expanding too quickly is that you just may not be able to handle the obligations of several locations or such a large corporation. Many of the larger corporations that have faced this have fallen through because of the enormous expense of taking on another building, another payroll, another unit.

Yet, the smaller business owner does not face this huge number of risks as the larger corporation. But!

It is important to make sure that you invest wisely in growth and not without investing time first. Determining where your potential benefits are is the first key to success. In addition, a good look at what the possibilities are is in order.

Are You Ready To Grow?

Those that are interested in finding the right solution in the terms of growth are doing the right thing. Remember though that it is important to make a decision in the right frame of mind and with the right amount of research done first.

In terms of growing, what the right choice is happens to be up to you individually. Ask these questions of your success:

1. Does your business have the cash flow to support not only this functioning location (or your current business) as well as another?

2. If you are expanding, what makes you believe that this expansion will serve your business well?

3. What is the likely expense of growing and does the business have the necessary means to protecting and covering that cost?

All of these things are crucial to your business's success in the growth factor. But, you also need to insure that you do not limit your growth with not enough opportunity either.

Don't Limit It

The mistake of many business owners is that they do not put their foot out there and expand fast enough or at all. While it is essential not to move too fast, it is just as important to consider if you are moving just too slow for benefit either.

To understand this factor, you again need to turn to your business. Are you getting all that you can from it? Can you do more or get a better bottom line if you do grow in some shape?

To learn the right amount of growth for your business, you can do test market studies, invest in surveys, or just start slowly and work up to it. The amount that you put into your business is really up to you and to how well the business has been doing to this point.

A bad business that is not doing well in one location may not be able to do well elsewhere either.

A good business that is thriving may be hindered by not moving it.

Of course, the opposite is true too. Research is the best way to determine where growth stands in your business.

Chapter 9: Managing Money Principles

What makes you profitable as a business owner? In the next chapter, we will look at the ways in which you must manage your cash flow and assets if you plan to have money in your pocket in the long term.

Do you have the ability to think about, analyze and then finally decide on business related decisions?

As we have discussed, your ability to do these things is what will hold you back or launch you forward today as well as well into the future. Now, take those ideas and determine just how well they fit into your ability to make decisions about your business success where it counts: the profit margin.

Throughout this chapter will we will talk about several aspects in detail, allowing you to fully understand what you need to do to be successful in regards to your business's profitability.

Controlling Your Money, Correctly

Do you have what it takes to manage your money? If not, it is time to find someone that can and will do it for you. Without tight control over the finances in your business, there is no telling what the future may or may not hold. That does not mean that you can not spend money. This is a huge mistake that people make.

Instead, as the entrepreneur and business owner, you need to learn to spend money the right way instead.

The first thing for you to do is to determine a budget for your business success. This should be an overall budget at first. Things to consider include:

- Managing expenses that will continue to keep the business up and running well.

- Managing your business's debt due to growth or to start up costs (to pay them down successfully.)

- Managing profit to if available must be done with an idea of how much will be spent on investing back into the business and what will go towards other beneficial needs the business has.

The budget should be done carefully, with a good deal of thought placed on each of these areas. Instead of a dollar mount, the budget of the business should be done by percentages.

Perhaps 20 percent of the profit will go towards investment back into the business whereas the rest of the profit will go to paying down debt. Whatever percentages you are comfortable with should be taken into consideration here.

Beyond the budget aspect of managing funds is the strictly organization aspects that need to be taken care of. Good quality, detailed accounting and bookkeeping needs to be done to manage the business's overall success and its funds to a "T".

In addition, there needs to measures put in place to manage unexpected expenses and even just making sure that everything is accounted for.

Although this seems obvious to note, plenty of businesses fail because of poor money management in the beginning stages. Do not get caught in the "I don't have time now, I will do it later" scam. Without doing this from the beginning, it will not happen throughout your business.

Don't Think You Need To?

If you do not think that you need to do this type of detailed accounting of your business, you are setting yourself up for a big failure. Now, that is not to say that you can not make a profit by being sloppy, but remember, we are talking about the long term here.

Even very large, international companies are very careful about where every penny that they spend goes. After all, this is money that could be doing something for the business, right? It does not matter if you have hundreds of dollars to budget or billions, tight money management is the key to successfully funding any business through good and bad times.

In addition, make sure you are monitoring these numbers as well. It does not do you any good to put in place a system and to use it but not to utilize it to the fullest extent. The fact is that you should be doing these things:

- Determine where money is going and if it is being done accurately.

- Determine where you can cut back in costs and expenses.

- Determine what you can do differently for less funds so without jeopardizing the actual quality of your business.

Being a bit tight wadded with your business is not a bad thing, assuming that you take care of all aspects of the business's need including reinvesting and growth potential as well.

Your Cash Flow

The next money management principal that you need to take into consideration is that of your cash flow. Without having a good amount of cash flow in your business, it will sink.

If you are a small business owner, it is even more important to do this simply because there is nothing and no one behind you to support that bad year or that big accident that has happened. Loans are only so good and they are not any good if you can not get them.

The ability to maintain your cash flow is the key to having a successfully and long term business. Without your careful management of cash flow, your business will not make it through leaner times or even the better times for that matter.

How do you do this? There are several things that you need to take into consideration here.

First off, you should make sure that as the entrepreneur you have a good strong hand in the cash flow of your business. You should be able to personally monitor it each and every day.

Does this sound like too much? If you do not do this, you can not possibly know where your business stands on any given day. That can lead to potential long term problems with your success.

Carefully consider each and every expenditure that you make. As an entrepreneur, you need to make these decisions wisely. Just as growing too fast can hurt you, so can not having the cash flow to support your business in the short or long term can.

In addition, you should personally monitor your budget, your expenses, your profit and your ability to use every dollar that you have wisely. That is what you have those budgets in place for, after all. Use them, keep at them and work each dollar to get the most out of it.

Two Principles to Remember

When it comes to business success, you will need to consider these two principles as far as how money management goes.

First, consider this: You should only be spending money when there is a potential to earn money from that expense.

It is self explanatory, isn't it? You should not be making an investment in your business, especially a small business owner, unless it will allow you to make more money as the end and direct result.

Secondly, consider this: "If it is not revenue, it is an expense."

How does that play into the business that you are currently running? Does it offer you the ability to make ends meet successfully? Do you make purchases without careful thought about those dollars? If it is not revenue to you, it is an expense.

Managing your cash flow successfully will allow your business to bank funds instead of to loose funds. When you do this successfully, your business has the potential to be a long term success. If you want to be there in the future, manage your cash successfully, with an eye on just about every dollar you have.

It's Not Being Cheap, It's Being Smart

Although it may sound like we are telling you to be frugal or cheap with your business, you need to insure that the funds that you are spending will be funds that are spent wisely, without waste.

How should you be frugal (that's a better name for it!) so much so that you will be able to find true success from doing so?

- Determine how you spend every dollar of your business's budget.

- Is that dollar being spent the best way that it can be? Does whatever it is being spent on benefit your bottom line?

- IS there a better way to spend that dollar? Can you get more for it with another company or service or another opportunity?

- Is there a way to save your money better, with a better return on it?

These are questions that any business owner should be considering each and every day that he owns his business. What can he do better to save more in his business for his business?

Why do this?

How many millionaires or even billionaires have you heard of that still drive their old, beat up cars? Why do they do that when they can afford to have much more beautiful and expensive cars?

It is not because they do not want to spend money or that they like being cheep. The benefit here actually comes from the fact that they like to save. Saving cash for your business is a great way to find true success because you will have those funds to use time and time again when you do need them.

The founder of Wal-Mart, Sam Walton, was worth $25 billion dollars at one point in his career. Would you believe that even with that type of worth he still drove his old, pick up truck into the job each day? Being frugal has its rewards as this is obviously what led him to having a net worth of $25 billion dollars.

When you are frugal, your business will prosper, year after year. If you are a spender, you won't have the funds to allow that to happen year after year, will you?

All of these money savings and cash handling tips may not seem like that big of a deal to you. If that is the case, you are already doing them and finding success with it, or you are actually wasting money and not achieving the success that you already want.

Yet, managing your funds wisely is one of the key components to your success in a small business. Every entrepreneur must take the time to do this or they will find themselves without the benefits that they need so badly.

In the end, is it worth being a bit frugal to reach that huge, multi billion dollar net worth? There is no car in this world that can make that type of promise to you, can it?

Make sure you install these money managing benefits and principals into your daily routine and long term goals within your business.

Chapter 10: Marketing For True Success

If you are an entrepreneur, marketing is something that is in your blood; at least it should be there if you plan to have customers at all.

Yet, do you market your business for true success and long term benefits?

If you think that you do, you may not truly understand the true potential of the right marketing tools.

What is marketing? Marketing is what draws a customer to your business. You need to let others out there know that you are there and ready and willing to provide a service to them.

That basic definition is not nearly enough to pull you through the entire process of marketing for your business success, though.

If you want long term success, take marketing much more seriously and follow these tips for various aspects of marketing.

Determine Your Product's Potential

Before you can be successful at marketing your business, you must take a good amount of time to determine what it is about what you have, that others do want.

In other words, what is it that your product provides? A successful business will offer some type of immediate satisfaction for a need that someone has. You should consider this even before you get into business. What is it that your product has the potential of solving or filling the need of?

In addition to this, you need to determine how it can offer these things to your customer in such a way as to better their life. Perhaps you can offer them something that solves a problem that they have but it still is something that is affordable to remedy that solution.

Having a clearly defined benefit to market is quite essential to getting the most from your product. People want to know, "What will it do for me?" and "Why should I purchase this over something else?"

When you can find out how this plays a role in your product's abilities, you can see the right course of marketing that product. Answering those questions is what you must do to find defined success here.

Pricing Matters Too

The next objective to take into consideration is that of pricing. When it comes to marketing, you may not think of the price that you put onto your product, but this does matter too. People are driven by sales and deals. They like a product that can provide them with the ability to solve their need but to do so in a cost effective manner.

Without the right pricing, it makes no difference how you market the product in the end.

What are people looking for when it comes to pricing of a product or service? They want something that is fair, not something that will cause them to go broke. In addition, most people understand full well that there is a need for the business to turn a profit. The problem comes when they are being taken advantage of.

In addition, competition matters here too. If your product is better than another, perhaps it should be more, but it shouldn't be outrageous because, if it is, no one will bother with it.

Take into consideration its ability to be called a Unique Selling Proposition. This means that it will have similar but at least some unique features that will allow it to be priced in competition to other products.

Of course, as we mentioned, your product must fill the need of someone out there. But, if there are five different products doing that, it can be hard for you to find your niche. Therefore, you must create for yourself a unique quality that will propel your marketing and your pricing.

What makes your product better, in other words?

If you are a new business owner, for example, and are looking for a new product to invest in, you may not want to try to come up with your own product, own service or other component. Rather, you may just decide that taking something that is already on the market and finding a way to make it even better, or better priced, is the right way to go.

Marketing Effectively

Throughout this chapter we have talked about ways that you can market your business successfully. Now, take into consideration your sales benefits.

Can you say that when each and every one of your employees (or just yourself) walks in the door their goal is to satisfy a customer?

Not just to serve a customer but to satisfy them as well. If you can not say that, then perhaps your marketing in sales terms is not working as effectively as it should.

Here's what we mean. If you plan to set out and make a profit, then your goal is to just make the most of the business you get.

But, what if you set out to please every customer? Then, you would not only be getting that sale, but you are also getting to keep that customer coming back time and time again.

Since we are talking about long term goals and success, it makes sense to insure that your goal in sales is to be the very best at what you to in order to please your customer so much so that he does not even consider going elsewhere for his needs.

In your business, you need to keep your marketing and sales techniques focused on creating as well as keeping your customer.

Sales for Success

Taking this one step further, you also need to take into consideration your sales abilities. As a successful entrepreneur, you need to carefully consider how you are selling, how effective it is as well as how you can improve it in the short and long term.

If you can not sell, you can not be successful in your business. Point blank, you are done.

First, as the business owner, you must be able to sell yourself. Are you the business person that is:

- Approachable
- Likeable
- Friendly
- Educated
- Dedicated?

Or are you the guy they all run away from when they walk into your door? Selling yourself as a trusted resource for information and product is the best way to become the go to guy.

In addition to this, you also need to effectively sell your product to your customer. This too goes along with marketing your business for success.

In short, if you can not sell your business successfully, then you have no business in business. Learn how to be excited with your own product. Then, learn how to successfully sell it to those around you.

You need to do this first before you encourage or train someone else to do it for you. Being eager, excited, positive and surely invigorating is the way to go in this case. If you do not feel comfortable talking about your product or business to your closest friends, how in the world can you sell it to a complete stranger?

Here's the bottom line of marketing and sales. If you can not be successful at getting your product out there and getting others to see it the way that you do, then you can not possibly find success with it.

Sales expertise is essential to sales happening. Having sales; means having customers that will come back to you. That equals long term success for you, as a business owner.

BONUS RECAP CHECKLIST

1. Start your business with your eyes geared towards your long term success.

2. Set and maintain goals that can be accomplished with long term objectives.

3. Manage growth carefully, without hindering your long term benefits.

4. Understand your market and how you belong in it.

5. Be the trend setter, cautiously.

6. Learn from both the good and bad of your past.

7. Invest wisely, decide wisely too.

8. Grow wisely without waste.

9. Manage your funds wisely, tightly, frugally, carefully.

10. Learn to market your business correctly, effectively.

BONUS #2

My associates and I have spent over $2 million developing the ideal system for entrepreneurs, teaching you ways to rapidly grow and expand your business. The platform is called the **E-Learning Marketing System**.

There are two things EVERY business owner wants. First, they want to generate more leads, attract more clients and make more money so they can eliminate any current financial distress they find themselves in. Second, they want to reach $1 million in annual revenue so they can begin to live the life they have always dreamed of having and so richly deserve.

The E-Learning Marketing System was specifically created to provide all small business owners with the tools, resources and support they need to accomplish both of these goals.

How? First, we help you target your ideal client, understand exactly what they want when they make their decision to buy, and create compelling marketing messages that enable you to out-market and out-sell your competition.

We even provide you with "done-for-you" marketing and advertising examples that are proven and tested to get real-world results. Once we help you to establish a successful and lucrative sales process, we then help you document this process and license it worldwide to others in your market.

With this system you receive:

- 52 weeks of video teaching covering in much more detail the principles discussed here
- Pre-written sale marketing copy to use immediately
- Custom designed flyers, brochures, and images for hundreds of businesses
- Regular weekly coaching calls
- A private virtual gathering with your peers, other owners who face the same challenges as you.
- Plus access to my private tools and tips for entrepreneurs.
- Plus much more

Because of the massive content, ready-made templates and content to blast your marketing efforts skyward, I usually charge $1,997 per year for membership to the site. This is a 15% discount over the monthly charge of $197.

Should you choose to engage my firm for helping you grow your business, you will be enrolled in this system for free.

Yes, you are welcome to join the system without using me as your coach. Just click to:

FindingTheEdge.com

Fill out the simple registration box on the right side of the home page. Someone from my team will be in touch.

Conclusion

In a world that is focused on the here and now, it is crucial for your own well being to keep an eye on your future.

When, you use wise business practices like the ones that we have talked about in this book; your goals wind up being quite beneficial. Not only can you find success for your business today, but the long term future of your business is more secured.

A business is an investment and it very much so can go either way (good and profitable or bad and costly.) When you start out on the right foot, providing the right tools, the right knowledge and a few principles for the way that you manage your business, you find yourself having more ability to head in the positive direction of your business.

It does not matter if your business is huge and worth billions of dollars or if it a brand new business barely off its feet. The goal is to give it the nurturing principles that can help it to grow and to prosper.

If you take the time to analyze, run, and then go back again and start all over each of these aspects in your business, the end result is success.

It is your money. You can spend it any way that you want to. Using these key principles will help you to have a successful business that adds dollars to your pocket over the years by maintaining a presence in the marketplace.

A business coach can help you work through these ideas. Rely upon someone who has been there, done that. I spent 20 years in banking, helping businesses grow. Then I spent another 20 years doing consulting and coaching to businesses of all sizes. I've been an entrepreneur, building 4 different enterprises amassing millions in gross revenue for me and my investors.

Now, I share this experience as a Master Coach, helping owners, founders, and entrepreneurs build their companies.

You can join my blog at

DougThorpe.com

or visit my company at

HeadwayExec.com

www.ingramcontent.com/pod-product-compliance
Lightning Source LLC
Chambersburg PA
CBHW060642210326
41520CB00010B/1713